Creative Classics

250 Playful Continuous-Line Quilting Designs

Laura Lee Fritz

C&T PUBLISHING

Text copyright © 2008 by Laura Lee Fritz

Artwork copyright © 2008 by C&T Publishing, Inc.

Publisher: *Amy Marson*

Editorial Director: *Gailen Runge*

Acquisitions Editor: *Jan Grigsby*

Editor: *Stacy Chamness*

Technical Editors: *Stacy Chamness, Georgie Gerl*

Cover Designer/Book Designer: *Christina Jarumay*

Junior Designer: *Kiera Lofgreen*

Production Coordinator: *Matt Allen*

Illustrator: *Tim Manibusan*

Photography by Luke Mulks and Diane Pedersen of C&T Publishing unless otherwise noted

Published by C&T Publishing, Inc., P.O. Box 1456, Lafayette, CA 94549

Library of Congress Cataloging-in-Publication Data

Fritz, Laura Lee.
    Creative classics : 250 playful continuous-line quilting designs / Laura Lee Fritz.
        p. cm.
    Summary: "250 continuous-line quilting designs based on classic quilting designs"
    --Provided by publisher.
    ISBN 978-1-57120-506-3 (paper trade : alk. paper)
    1. Quilting. 2. Quilts--Design. I. Title.

TT835.F7574 2008
746.46--dc22

                    2007034782

Printed in China

10 9 8 7 6 5 4 3 2 1

Contents

What You Can Do With These Designs

Add beauty and special meaning to your quilting projects by using the graceful continuous-line images shown in the following pages. Whether you are quilting by hand, home sewing machine, or with a long-arm machine, this collection of designs will be a generous resource library. Combine them with each other and with interesting background-filling textures. Enlarge or reduce any of the designs to use on your quilts, and feel free to arrange and combine these ideas with more of your own.

Planning the Design

If you think of your quilt in terms of a stage, and the quilting designs as the actors on that stage, designing your overall quilting plan will be easy. One design will act as the lead character on center stage, with a supporting cast of one or more secondary design ideas. Provide some backdrops, such as a background grid and some architecture, and your story will unfold.

Transparent designs combine interesting shapes but they are not made up of recognizable imagery. An overall meandering is an example. Because of their simplicity, "transparent" designs don't jump out at you as you study a quilt. You can combine recognizable images with transparent designs, such as an oak leaf "floating" in still waters.

Transferring Designs

If you aren't ready to make the leap into free-motion quilting, there are simple methods to transfer the designs onto your quilt top.

Paper or Tulle

Trace the designs onto paper with a black permanent pen so you can use a copy machine to resize any image for your block or border. Trace the design again onto stencil plastic and cut it out.

You could alternately trace the design onto tulle, then draw through the tulle onto your quilt top.

Both of these methods are a means to draw directly onto your quilt top with chalk, washout pencil, clean-erase pencil or a water/air soluble pen.

Water-soluble Stabilizer

You can also trace your designs onto water-soluble stabilizer with a water-soluble pen and quilt through it as the topmost layer of your quilt. Try the Solvy stabilizers made by Sulky, or Dissolve from Superior Threads, as they really do wash out of the cloth.

Washable Marker

Another option is to trace directly onto your quilt top with a washable marker.

Draw the designs onto paper with a black permanent pen and use a copy machine to resize them for your block or border. Clean white paper and bold black drawing lines will project best through the cloth.

Make your own light box by placing a glass panel over a quilt frame or sawhorse set, then placing a light source such as a four-foot fluorescent shop light below the "table." Now spread your quilt top on the glass and turn the light on. Slide your drawings under the quilt, and position as desired. Trace these designs directly onto your quilt top with a washable marker.

Border Designs

Once you choose a border design, you have three decisions to make: what direction to face the design; how to space or fit the border pattern to the length of the fabric border; and what to do in the corners.

Consider the direction the borders will be viewed. A wall quilt's borders all have the top of the design facing the same direction. A throw quilt might have the borders all facing outward, or inward. A bed quilt may look great with a top border design's top to the head of the bed; the lower border also having its top to the head, and side borders top to the middle so they are right side up when viewed from the sides.

Fit the border images within the span of the border. If the length of fabric would cause you to end mid-image, then choose a tight spot between two images to extend a simple line an extra ¼″–¾″ to spread the border. Repeat the spread each time you come to the same repeat in the border. This means doing a little math: If you need 4″ more on a border design that is repeated nine times, then add ½″ between each repeat. In the same manner, you can shrink space between images, and repeat the shrinkage each time you come to a repeat of the place you compacted the design. The spread or compaction may be different for the side borders than for the top/bottom borders, as the border length will be different.

An alternative to spreading or shrinking is to divide the border design in half, with half of it facing the opposite direction, creating a mirror image. If you choose this route, add an extra design in the middle, between the border designs.

Add corner designs to provide a transition between the horizontal and vertical borders. Ideally, one of the images in the border will fit the corner block. You may draw a simple curved connecting line between each of the two borders, sometimes getting a bit creative when choosing where to connect the lines. You may choose a feature image or a background image, or possibly draw a new version of some idea in the border.

Start Quilting

Practice your machine quilting in order to find your rhythm, and learn to sew at a constant speed.

Sewing a Continuous-Line Quilting Design

Note any pattern sections where you change sewing direction, sew over an area twice, or sew over an existing line of stitching. You may find it helpful to draw arrows using a high-lighter marker on the pattern to guide you.

For most of the patterns the starting and stop-ping points are indicated. You can start at either end of the pattern and sew left to right or right to left.

When you start or end a line of quilting, or when your top thread or bobbin is depleted, knot the end(s) of your stitching line and thread a needle with the thread tails. Use a long-eye sharp embroi-dery needle for the tail so both threads will fit through at once. Try wrapping the pair of threads around the eye tightly, pinch the thread to hold the tiny loops as you withdraw the needle then slip the eye over these tight little loops. Sew these ends by sliding the needle back along your quilting line, pull the needle out, bury the knot into the batting, and cut the tail.

Clowning Around with the Clamshell

We know clamshells as a quilting *pattern*, but let's take a look at its possibilities as a *format*, a plan for the organization and arrangement of quilting.

Start with a row of round hills, build a second row staggering—or offsetting—the row of hills. This is the classic clamshell.

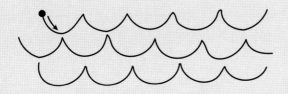

Top row first.

Bottom row first.

Let's define the format: the low points of one row "kiss" the highpoints of the next and previous rows.

Apply the format to a thundercloud concept.

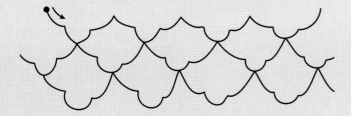

. . . or to a simple V . . .

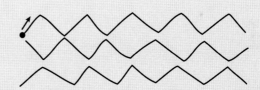

. . . or to a complex V.

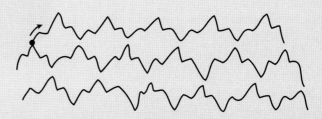

Now, some new ideas:

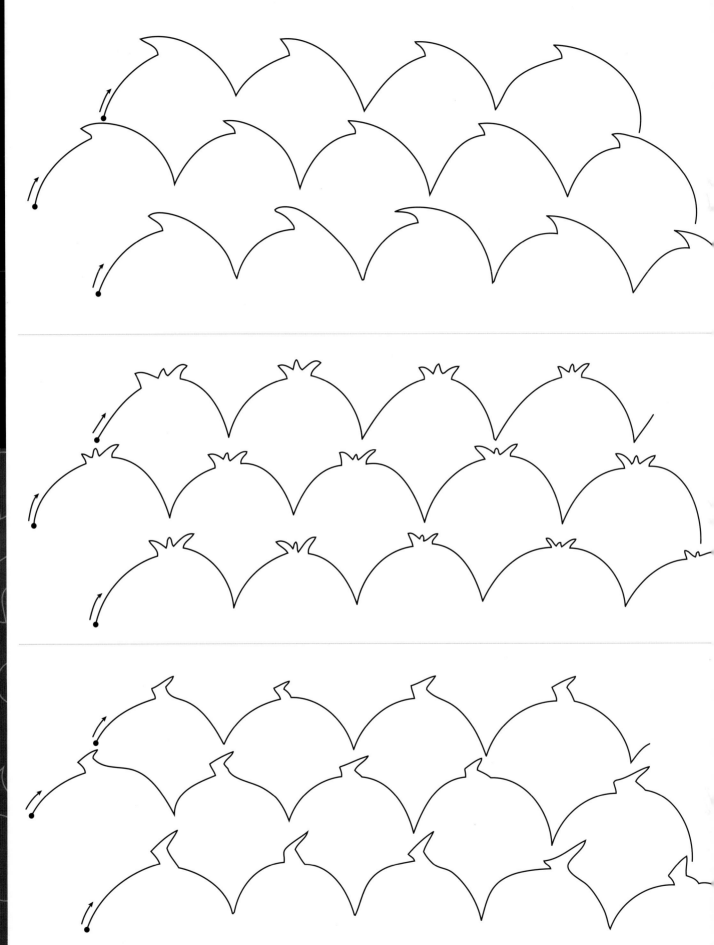

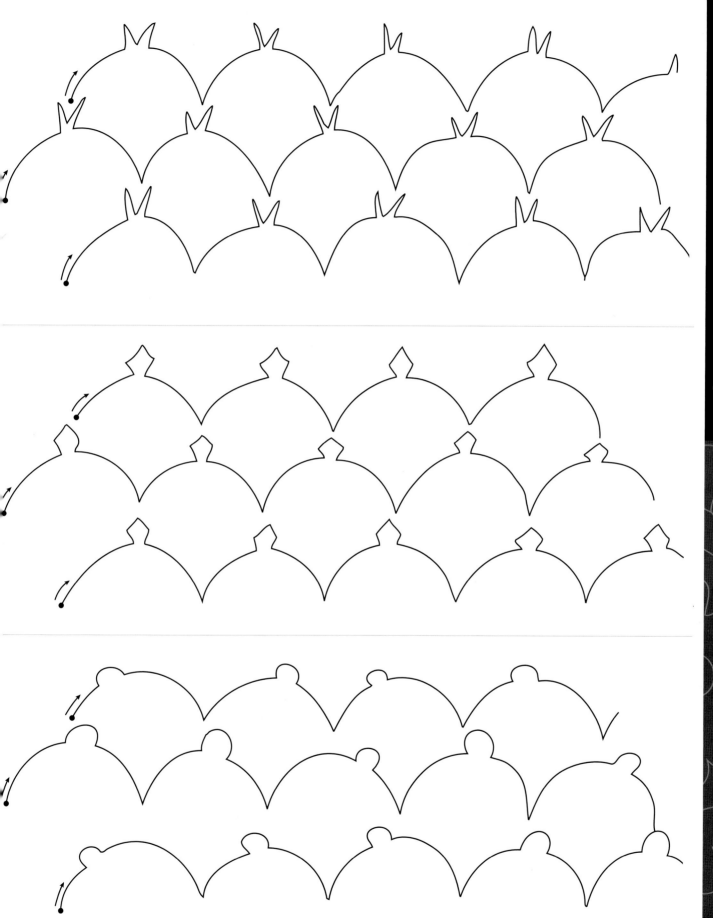

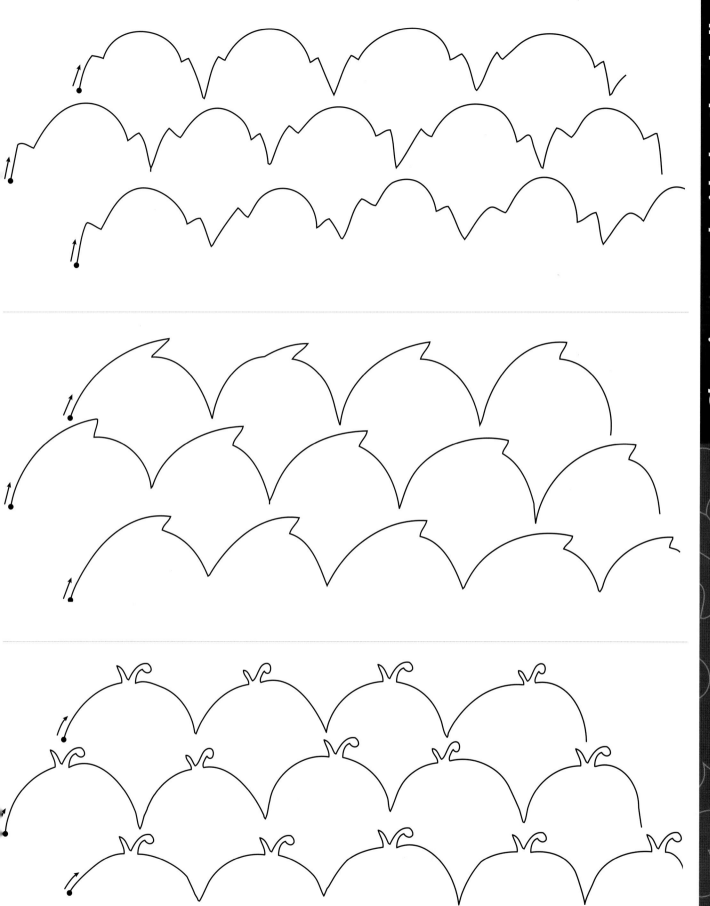

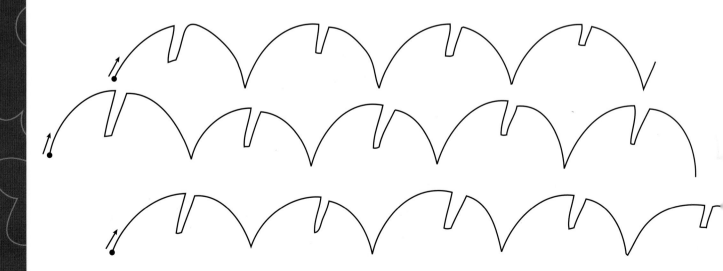

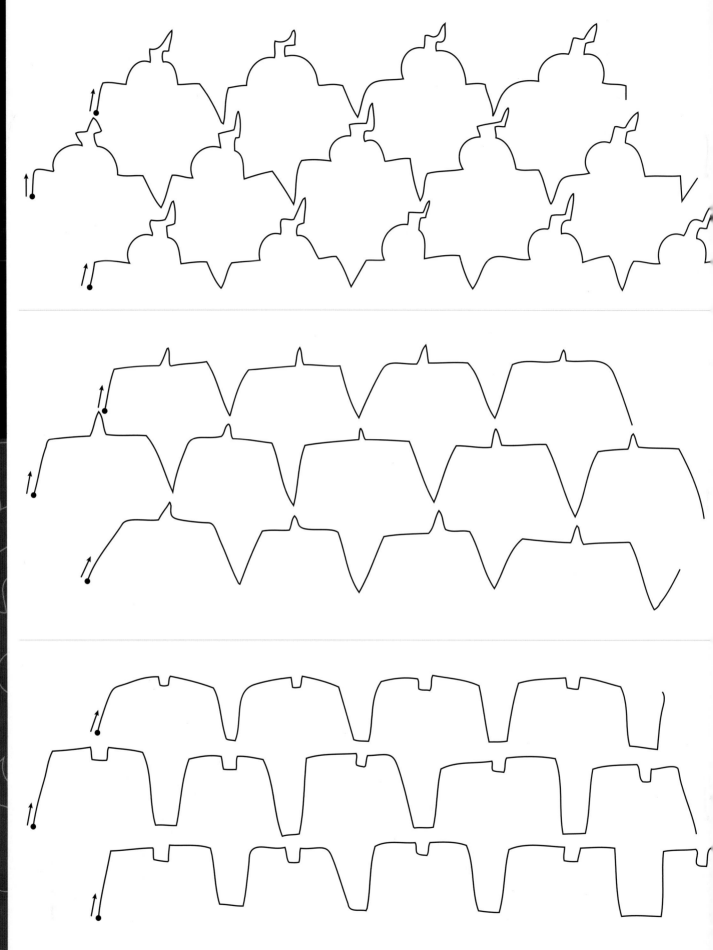

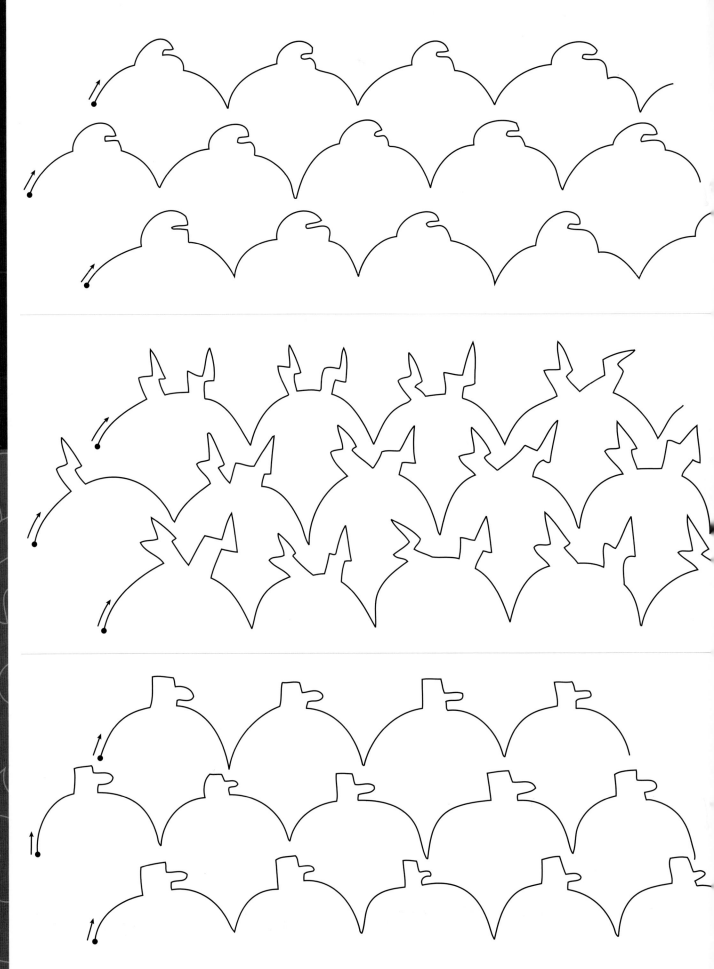

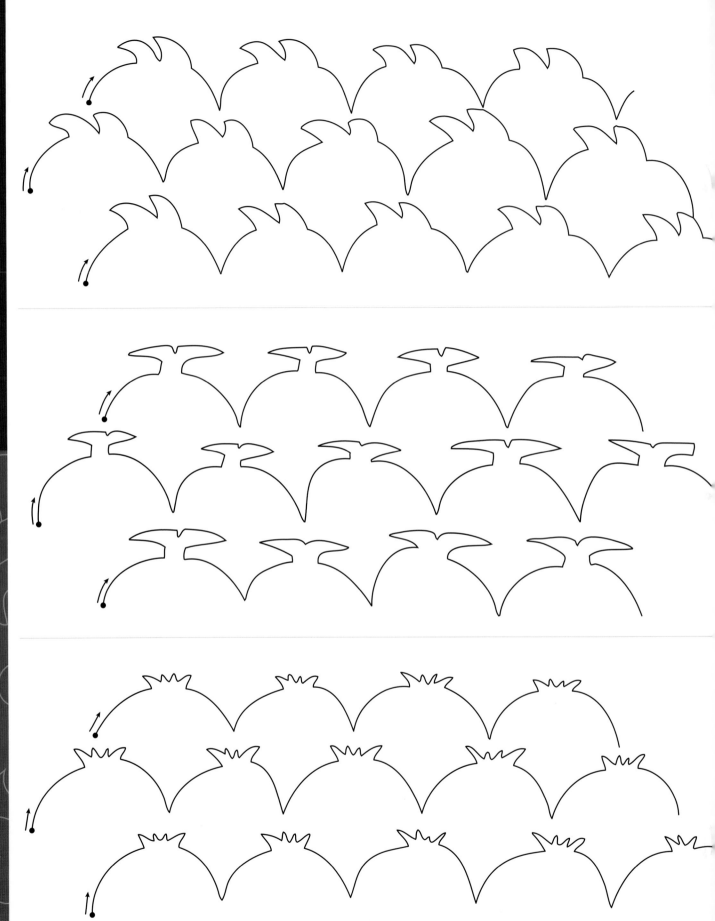

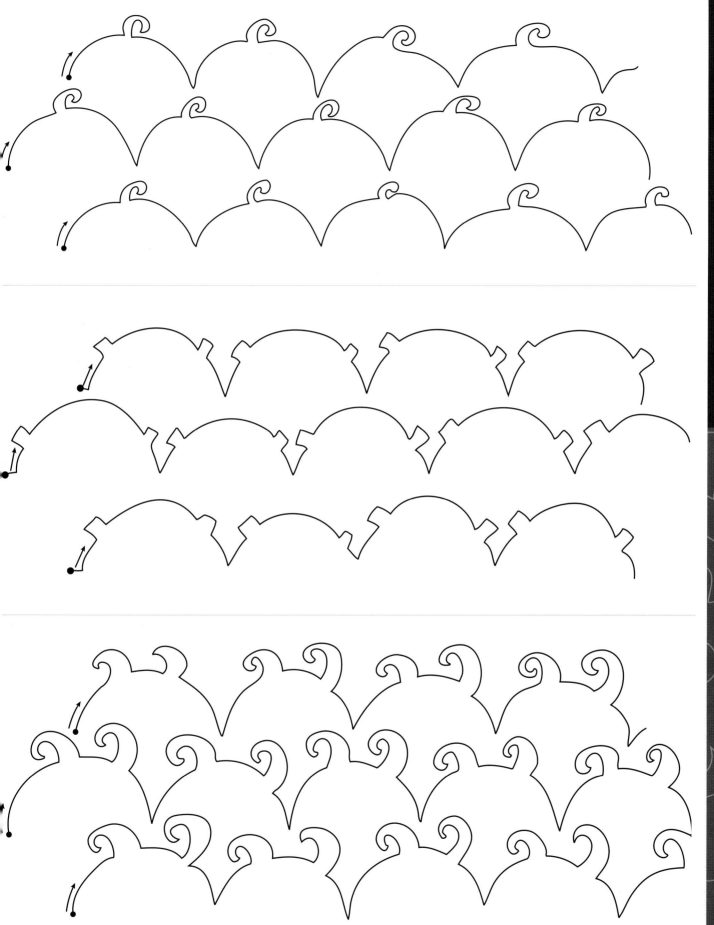

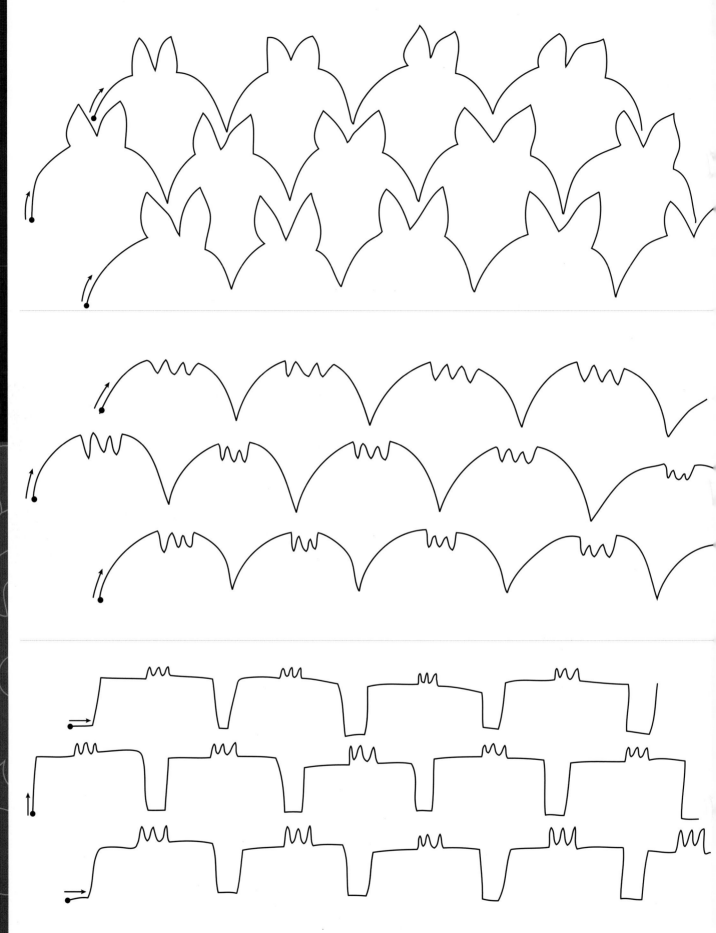

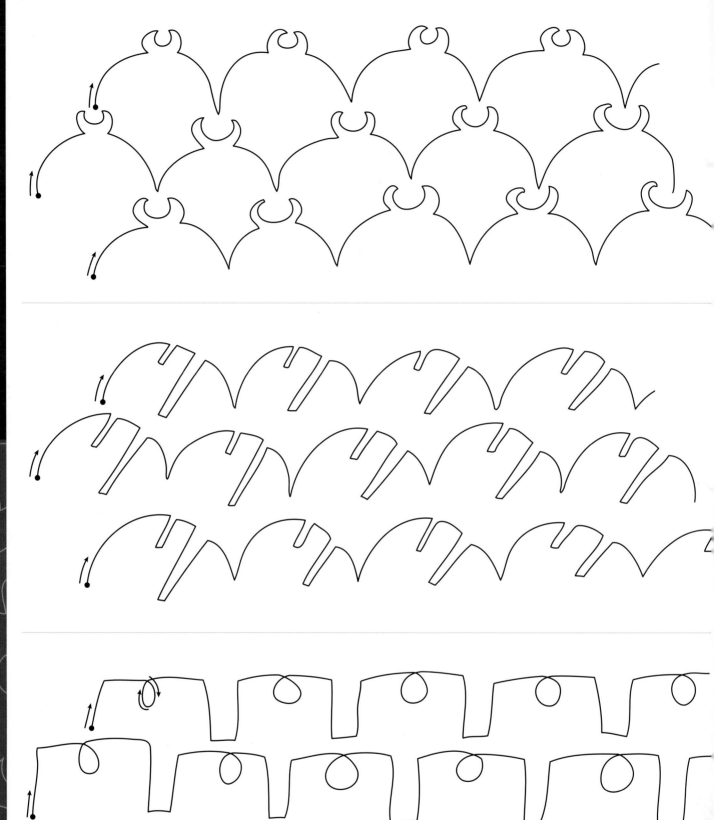

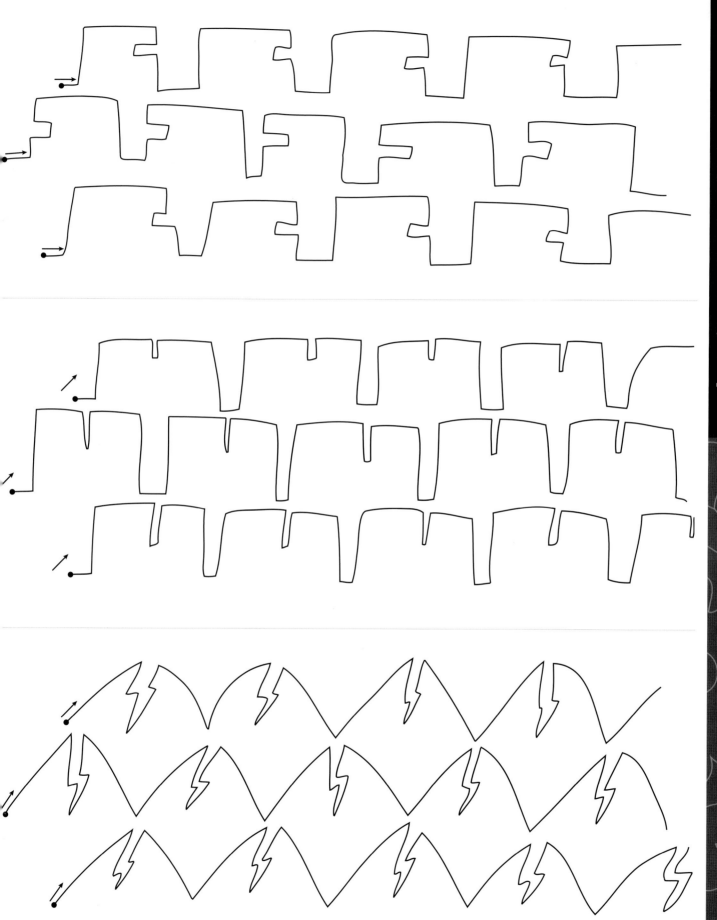

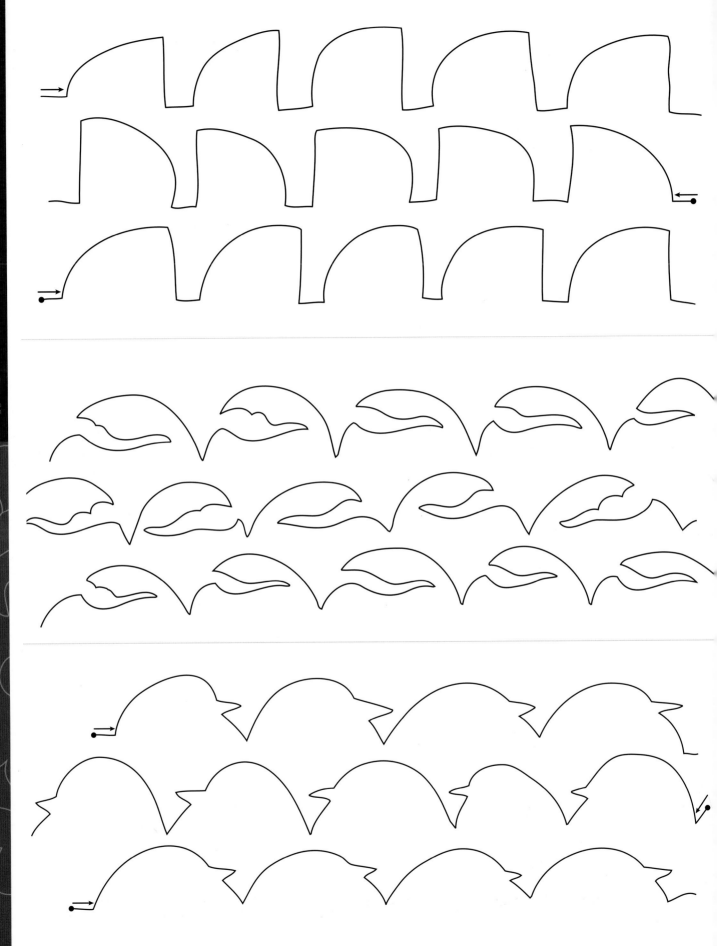

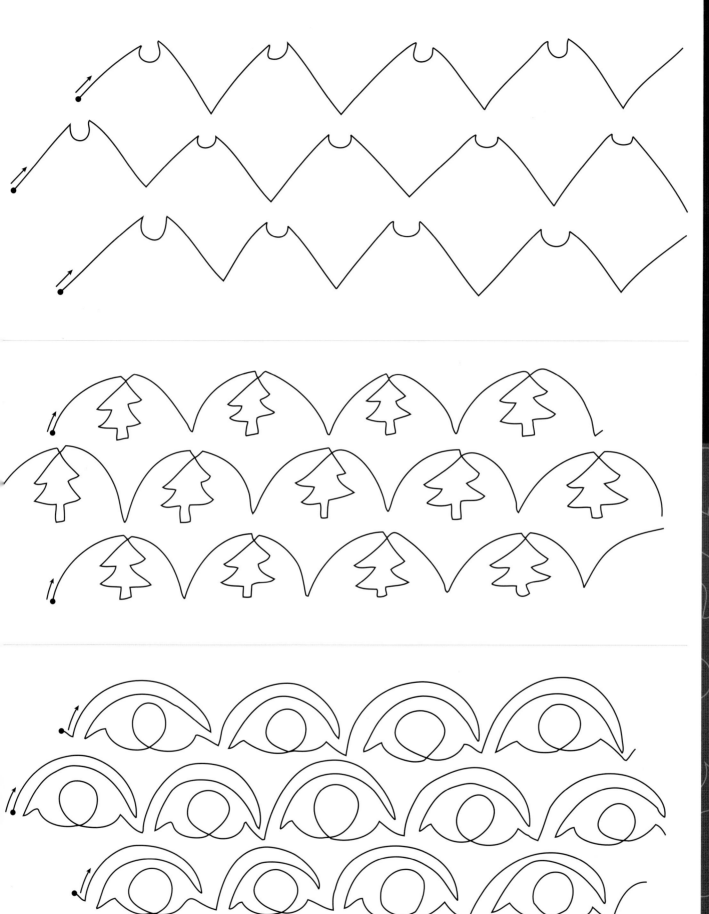

29

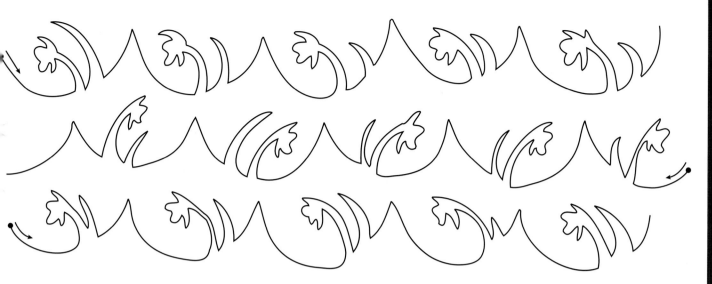

Worldly Waves

An easy wave pattern to fill a narrow border—or doubled and offset for a wider border—
is a common quilt design:

the offset row

A bit of exaggeration will turn it into a classic rope design.

Look at the wave as a format for drawing new designs. Start with a row of waves and add
a small or elaborate variation.

A single row of course will be a border. Sashes will not be drawn with a wave format generally,
as the wave does have two distinctly different effects—thin at the top, voluptuous below. A sash
needs to interact with adjoining blocks in the same manner, as I illustrate here.

Both edges have matching
negative space.

Same negative space

Same negative space, same design effect.

thin and spikey wave top

round and full wave bottom

A two-sided design will seem off-balance as a sash, but you can carefully frame blocks in a decided manner.

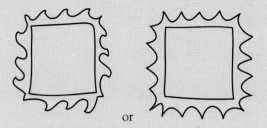

or

This is what I mean by framing blocks.

Wave designs can be identical repeating rows, or offset in alternating rows.

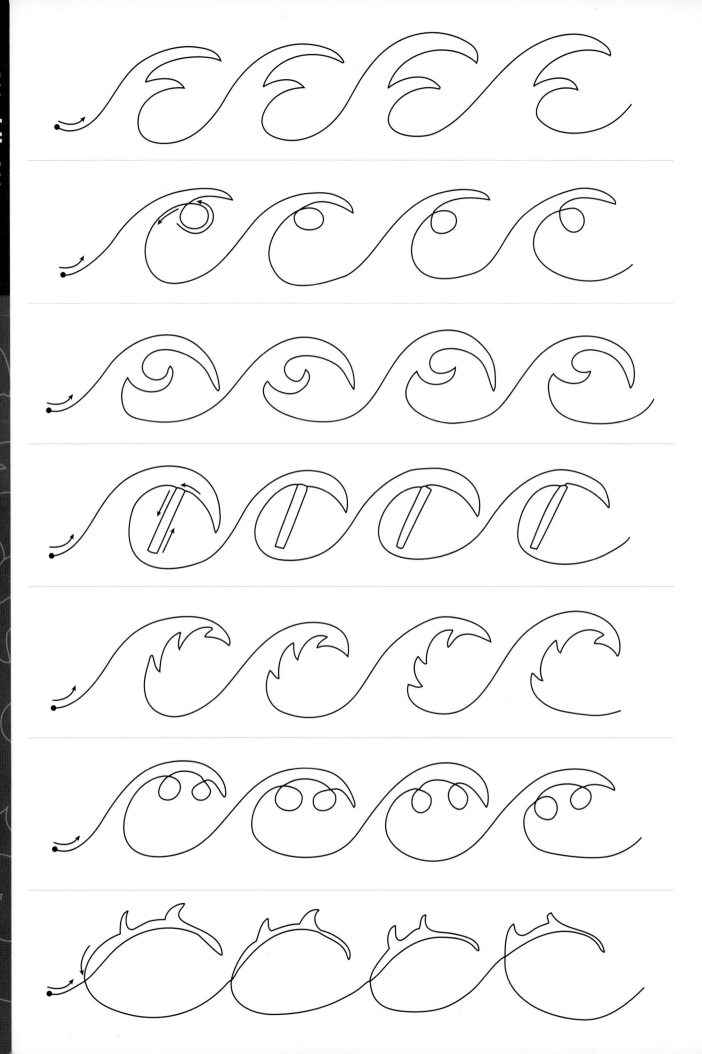

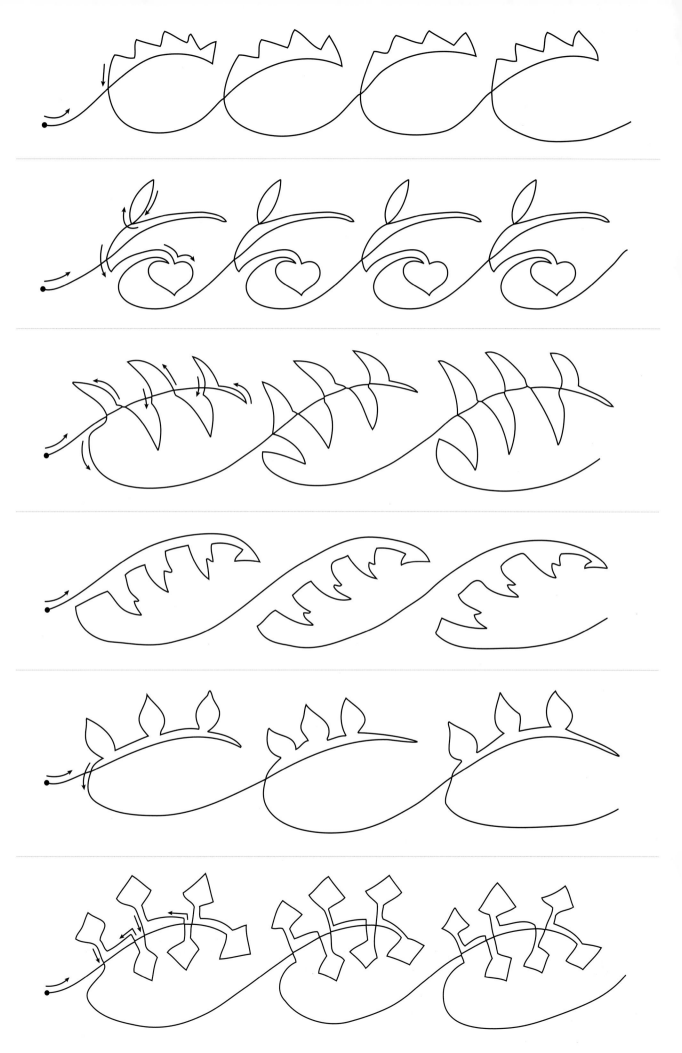

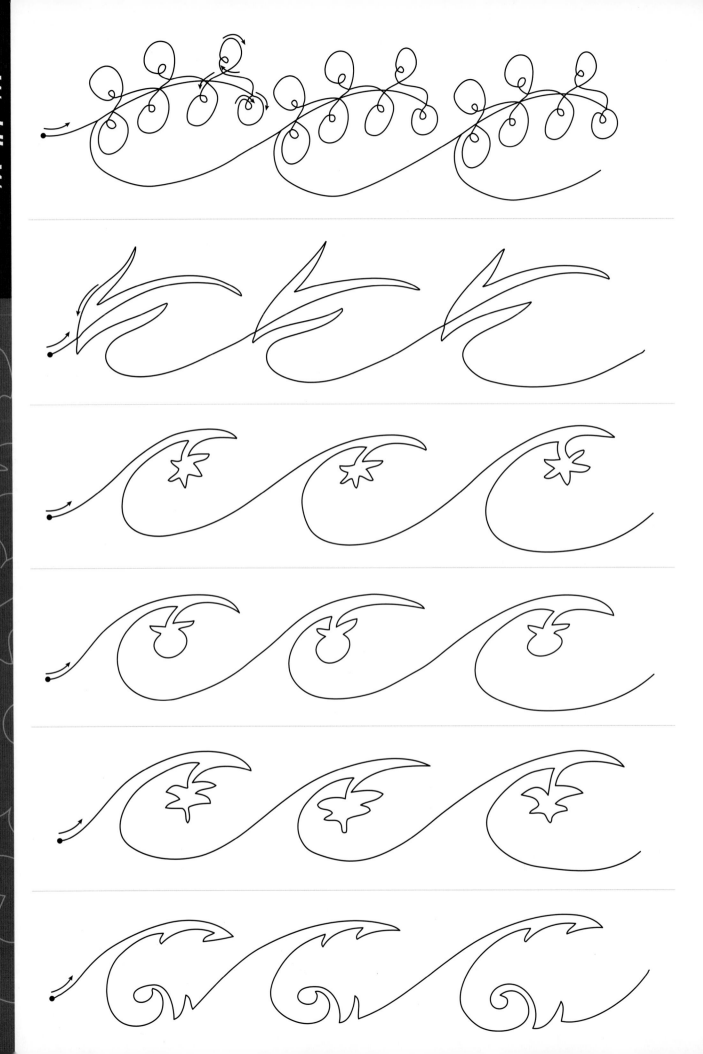

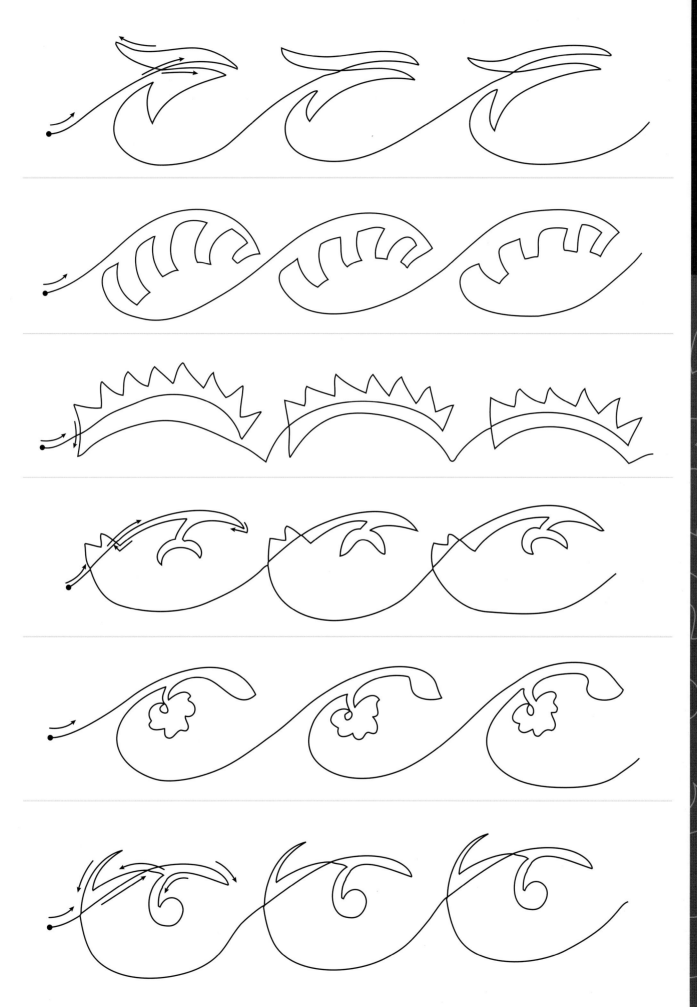

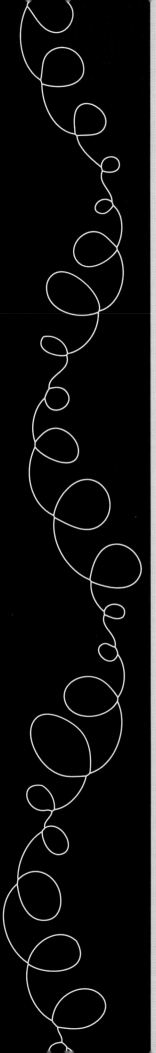

Scintillating Serpentines

While a serpentine line is indeed a good spine for creating feather designs, here are some excellent examples of other ways to make use of such a simple format.

Serpentine line

Perfect for a very narrow border, say ³/₄˝ to 1˝, this shallow-humped serpentine has an "accidental" leaf detail.

The leaf detail not only decorates the line, it distracts you from noticing whether or not the curves are precisely measured and matched. As a fan of the human touch, I tend to make a distinction between the concept of perfection and precision. For all the costly effort many of us spend to attain precision in our quilting, we don't gain any more perfection than does the quilter whose work has a cockeyed block or a bit of "make it do" in a quilt.

Practice "finger drawing" designs before you mark your quilt or start your freehand quilting. Tracing your finger over the design two or three times helps to make you more familiar with how the design flows. In turn, when you actually quilt it, your work will be more fluid.

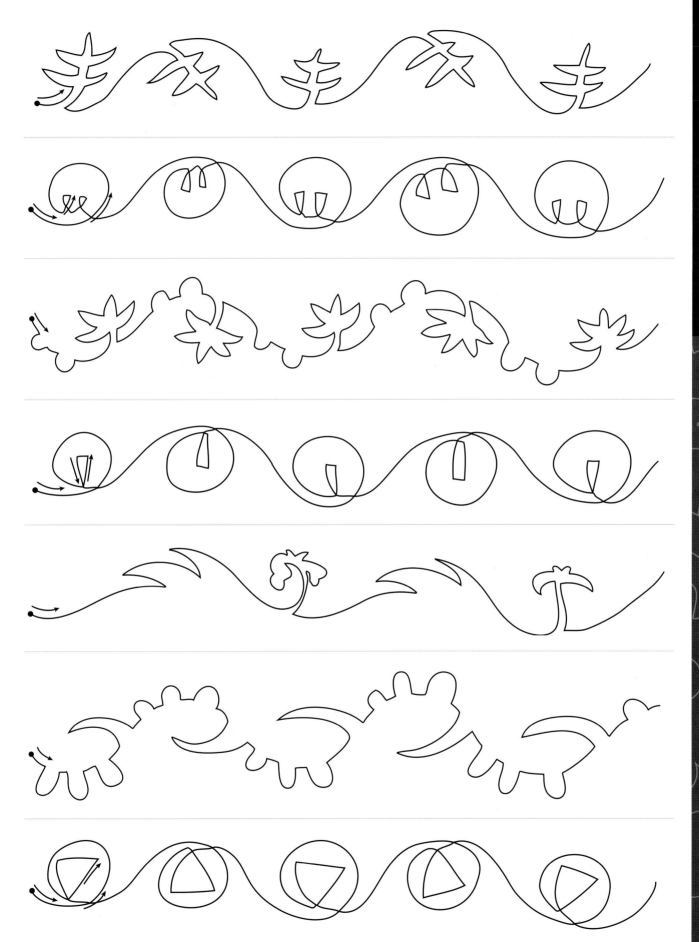

Be-Bop the Baptist Fan

Draw against the edge of a plate to get the arc, and draw against it again just inside that arc. This is the basis of the Baptist Fan quilting design. It is one of the most-recognized classic patterns, usually traveling at random across a quilt. To make it travel fluidly in machine quilting, it is begun at the center of the nesting arcs, with the smallest arc. Continue an arc until it "hits" another line or an edge of the quilt, echo that line or edge for a short distance—½" maybe—and begin the next arc. Always keep going until you bump against that next field. Just shy of the collision I stop, at a distance equal to the space between arcs. When complete, this creates the illusion of another arc. When you choose, otherwise, to go completely to the next line, the sewn result is a consistent yet inter- mittent double-line quilting area. Neither is right or wrong, but make it a choice, not an accident.

Here is a visual comparison:

This is with the space

This is with the doubled line areas

In this example I am creating a border-type design— it is traveling to the side with unmatched shapes along the top and bottom of the border. I braid it, so both sides are identical for a sashing:

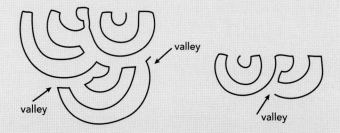

To make the Baptist Fan travel across a quilt as a random overall pattern, start from the smallest arc and make the concentric arcs until they are no longer smooth to sew. When you reach a size that wobbles instead of arcs, start a new small center arc. By the second or third time you start a new "rainbow" you will start to see "valleys" to use for your starting places.

valley

valley

valley

Do not make a loop or a hook unless it is part of an intended variation. Just make a smaller version of the same shape. Any extra turns of the line will look out of place—of course, with beauty and repetition it will become its own pattern.

Either a doubled center arc, or an extra-long reach or a hooked echo will get you out of a tight spot—all are out of character for the design.

This design illustrates some difficulties for a flowing overall pattern; the long petal fills space so quickly there's no room to wiggle over to another area in pattern.

> **Tip**
> *Mix large and small sizes throughout the design so you never get stuck where you can't get out.*

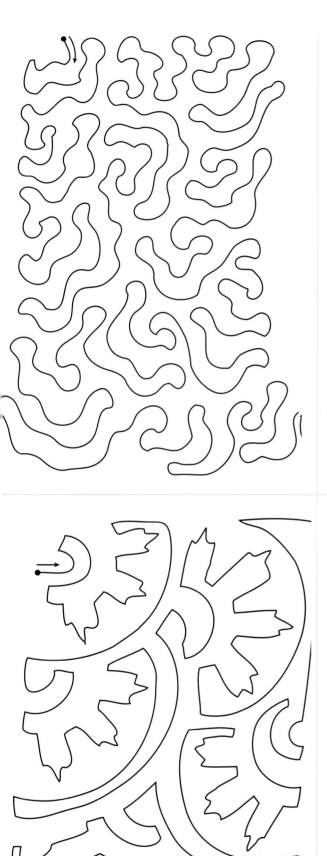

Aim for making the petals the same size,
this is not an echo pattern.

If you need to head in the other direction,
cover the petal row with a smooth arc or two.

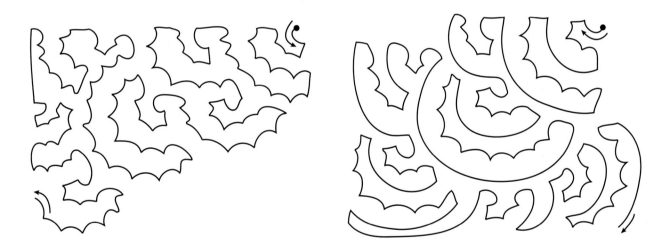

Compare these designs.

Those long, reaching lines will make a pattern—
be sure it doesn't begin to dominate the view.

Switching directions on petal tips takes longer to quilt.

Flaunting the Feathers

The classic feather quilting design is much loved by those who feel precision is equal to perfection. I find that these two concepts often cancel each other out, and that perfection can be found in the unique and askew production of the unsteady, but searching, hand.

Let that thought launch this study of the feather as a format—not a pattern. Feather designs have a curvy spine with plumes on both sides of the spine. Much has been written about making those plumes in the most aesthetic shape but I'll show you ideas that will launch you into finding yet more variations for those plumes than I can put to paper here. So, let's flaunt the feather!

What to do about the spine?

For a border or sash, a serpentine curve will do—a narrow border gets a shallow curve.

A wide border can also get a shallow curve—the plumes will reach to the right edges of the border, no matter how shallow or deep the curve.

A shallow spine in a large border

A deep spine in a large border

Spines curving to fill blocks; let the spine flow, then fill the space.

Tip
Before you flaunt the rules, it makes good sense to master them.

A lovely plume will nest into the next, and will have a voluptuous tip and a long trailing tail virtually echoing the spine.

It can be a mental juggle to make one side of plumes left to right and the other side right to left. If any of the following designs are difficult to stitch, just double the spine.

Now you know all the rules. So, now you can break them. Here are 75 imprecise plumes—or ways to use the feather as a format.

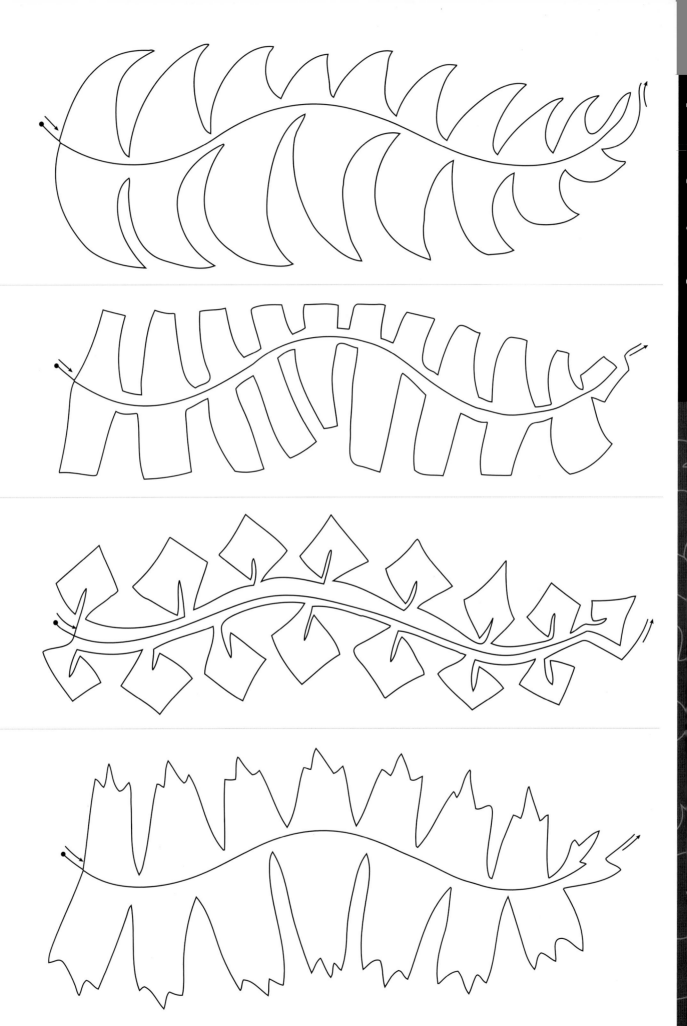

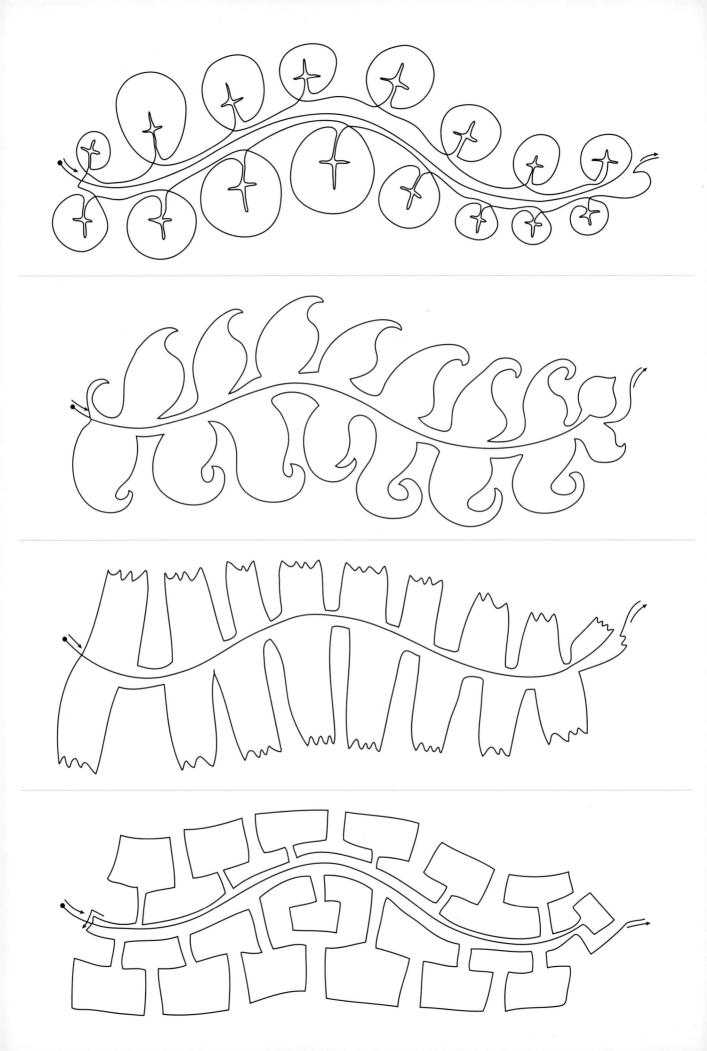

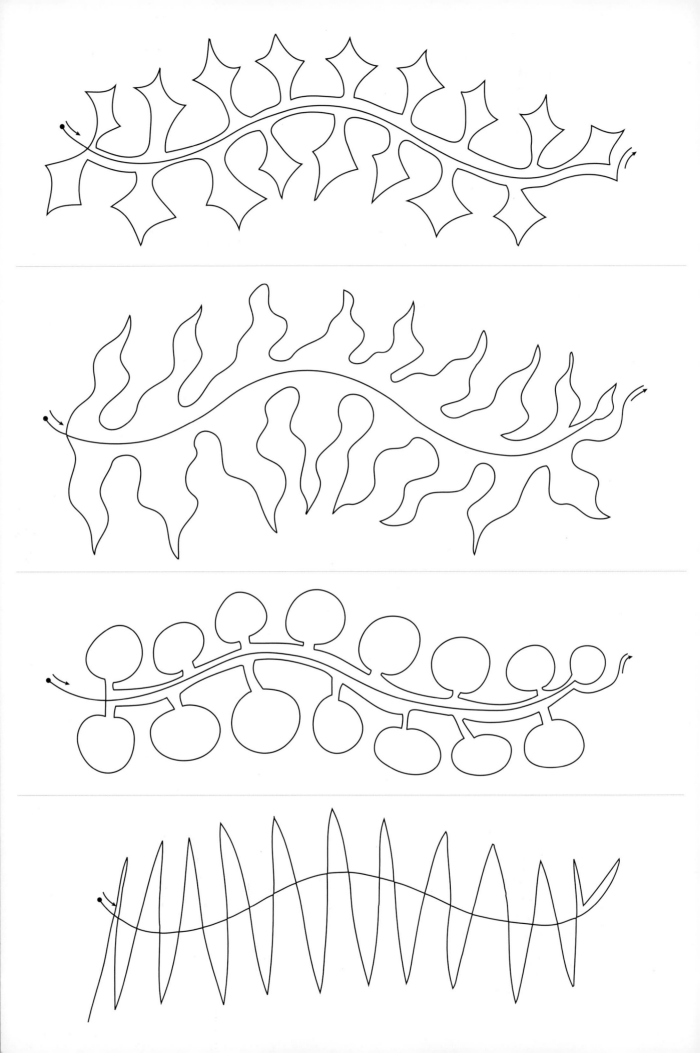

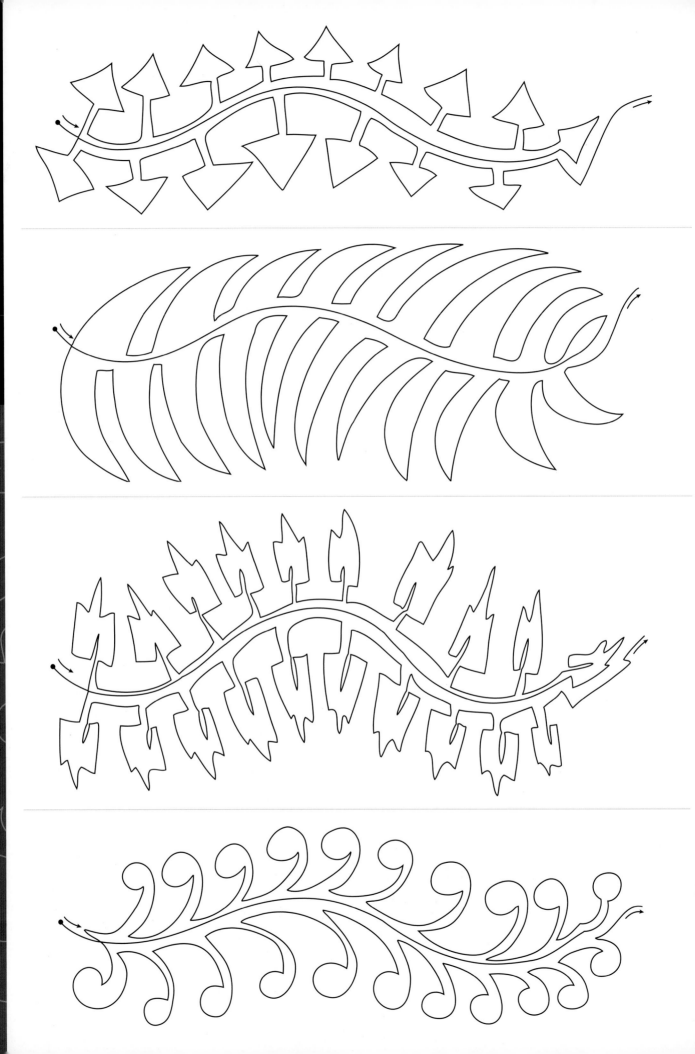

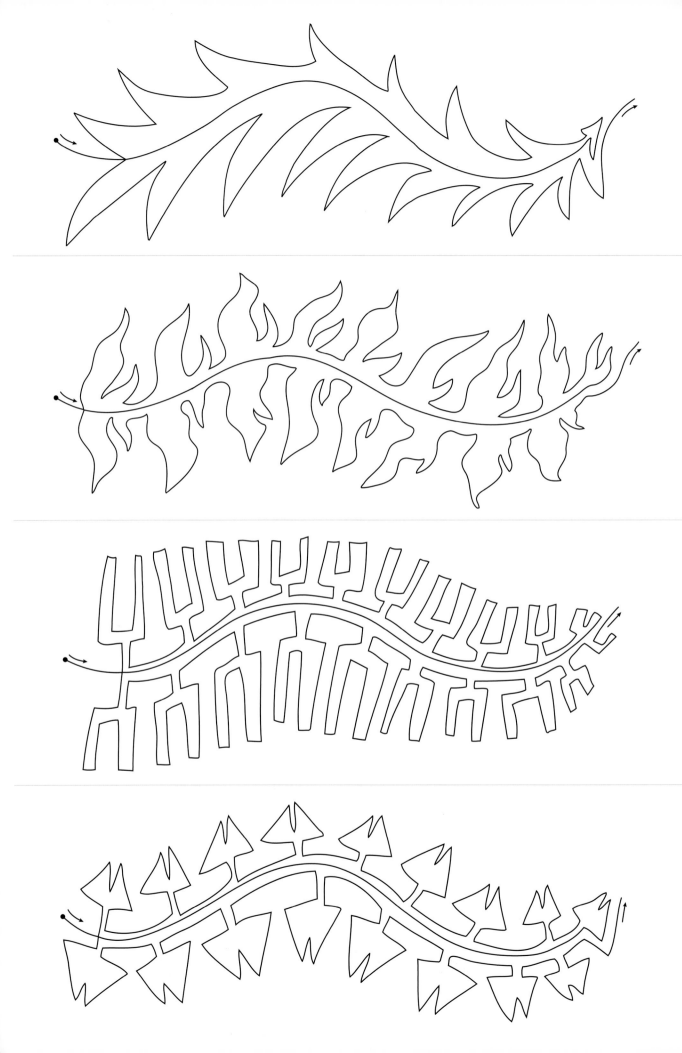

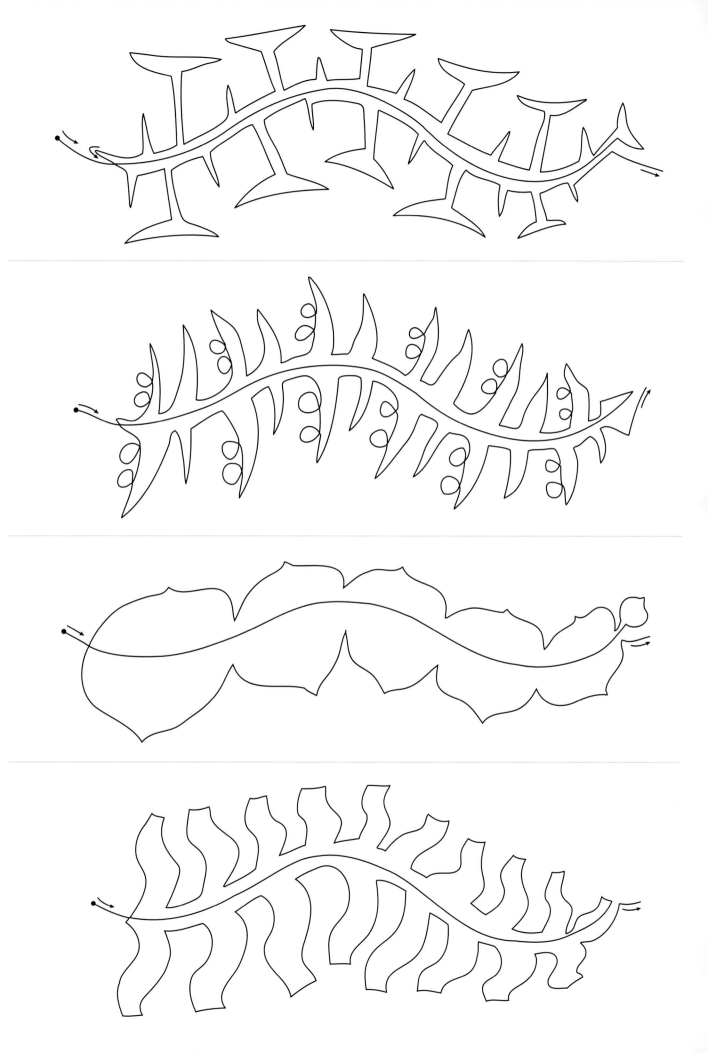

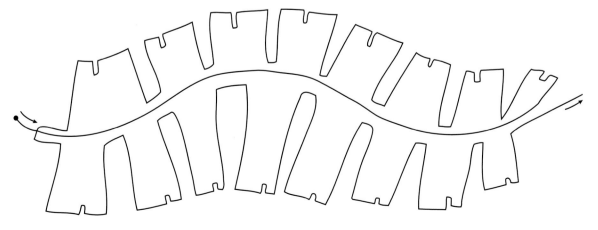

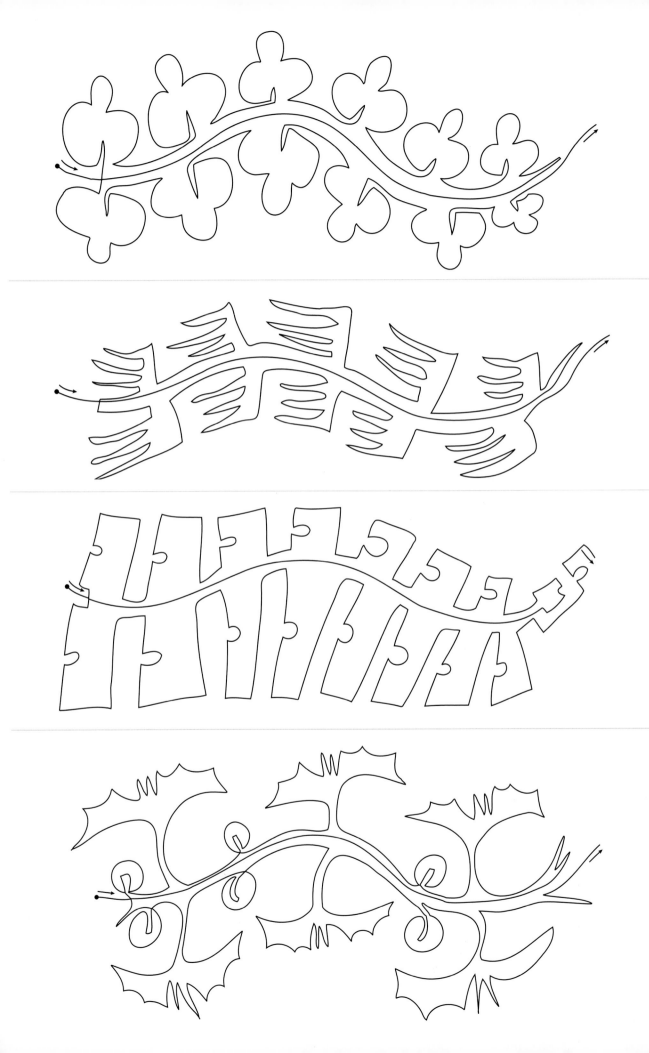

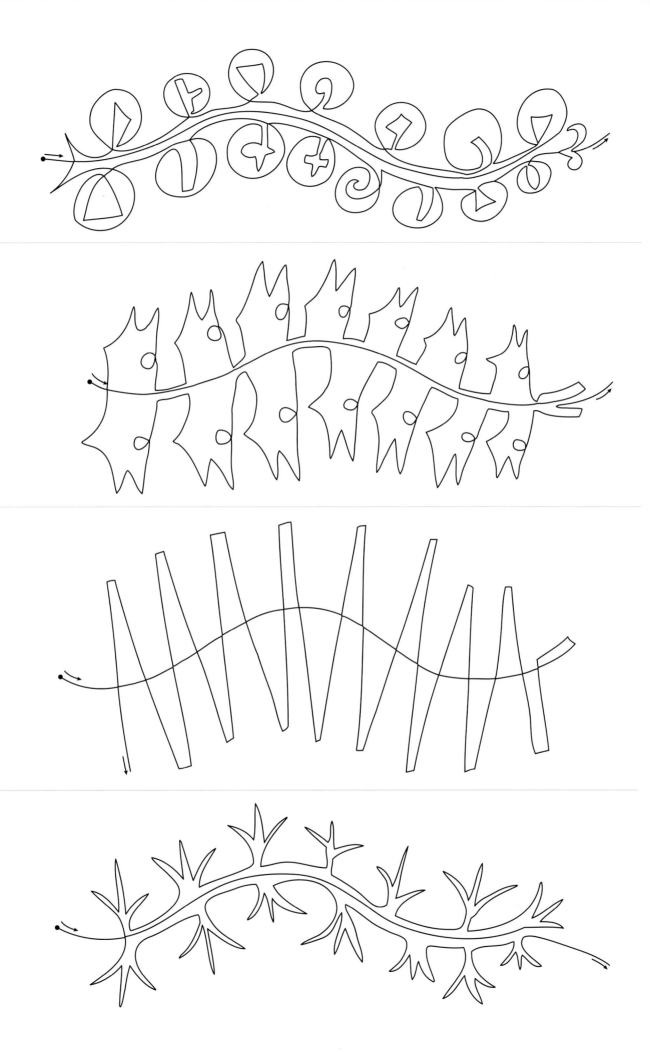

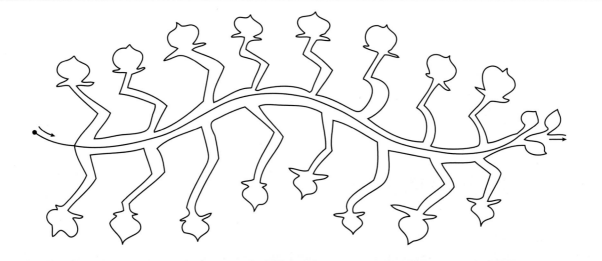

About the Author

Laura Lee Fritz is widely known for her hand appliqué quilts and her fanciful wholecloth quilting filled with narrative images from the stories surrounding her life. Laura raises bluetick hounds and Navajo-Icelandic sheep in rural Bitterroot Valley, Montana, but slips off of the farm to teach quilting classes from Napa Valley College in California to her long-arm machine quilting classes at the annual International Quilt Festival in Houston. Drop in to see her quilting machine shop Houndholl'r Quilting, in a log cabin at the south edge of Missoula on Highway 93.

Laura Lee Fritz
Houndholl'r Quilting
P.O. Box 846
Lolo, MT 59847
877-779-2435

A Word About Art

Being an artist is all in the practice of art. Those of us who make pretty lines attract people who value pretty lines. If we create bold, abstract lines we attract those who value that form. Folk art is a more spontaneous art form; we just need to make the story unfold. There are vast numbers of people who are attracted to folk art for its direct simplicity. Throughout history, quilts have represented people's lives, often expressing a love of story as well as love of color.

It is sufficient to practice your craft in an expressive way, and follow the path of just "doing it." You will begin to see the world with a greater attention to what it truly looks and feels like, and those observations will appear in your work. Now you are an artist.

Resources

Batting

Hobbs Bonded Fibers
200 South Commerce Dr.
Waco, TX 76710
800-433-3357
www.hobbsbondedfibers.com/quilters.html

Quilter's Dream
589 Central Drive
Virginia Beach, VA 23454
888-268-8664
www.quiltersdreambatting.com

The Warm Company
5529 186th Place SW
Lynnwood, WA 98037
425-248-2424
www.warmcompany.com

Quilting Frames

Flynn Quilt Frame Company
1000 Shiloh Overpass Rd
Billings, MT 59106
800-745-3596
www.flynnquilt.com

Gammill Quilting Systems
1452 West Gibson
West Plains, MS 65775
800-659-8224
www.gammill.net

Handi Quilter
76 S Orchard Dr.
North Salt Lake, UT 84054
877-MY-QUILT (697-8458)
www.handiquilter.com

Threads

American & Efird, Inc.
P.O. Box 507
Mount Holly, NC 28120
800-453-5128
www.amefird.com

Superior Threads
87 East 2580 South
St. George, UT 84790
800-499-1777
www.superiorthreads.com

YLI Corporation
1439 Dave Lyle Blvd. #16C
Rock Hill, SC 29730
803-985-3100
www.ylicorp.com

For a list of other fine books from
C&T Publishing, ask for a free catalog:
C&T Publishing, Inc.
P.O. Box 1456
Lafayette, CA 94549
800-284-1114
ctinfo@ctpub.com
www.ctpub.com

For quilting supplies:

Cotton Patch
1025 Brown Ave.
Lafayette, CA 94549
800-835-4418 or
925-283-7883
Email: CottonPa@aol.com
Website: www.quiltusa.com

C&T Publishing's professional photography
services are now available to the public.
Visit us at www.ctmediaservices.com.

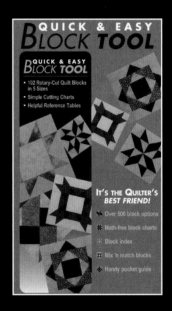
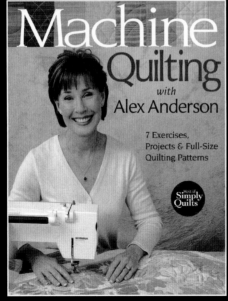
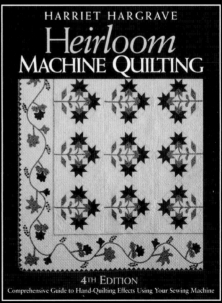